C000148111

HOW TO SELF-PUBLISH
YOUR CHILDREN'S PICTURE
BOOK USING POWERPOINT

Copyright © 2017 **Karlene Stewart**

All Rights Reserved. No part of this publication may be reproduced, stored in a retrieval system, or transmitted in any form, without the express consent of the author. The only exception is by a reviewer, who may quote short excerpts in a review.

Visit the author's website at
http://www.karlenestewart.com/

CONTENTS

Who Is This Book Written For?..1

Why Me? 3

Chapter 1 - Children's Picture Book Vs. Children's Story
Book 4

Chapter 2 - Planning Your Book............................8

Chapter 3 - Text Choice And Design............................19

Chapter 4 - Publishing 44

You're Published 62

Thank You 63

About The Author 64

WHO IS THIS BOOK WRITTEN FOR?

Have you written a children's picture book? Are you eager to get it published but don't know where to begin? Well, read on, as this book is for you. Completing your picture book manuscript is a great start, but that's only the beginning of the process to having your published picture book.

This book is for anyone looking for guidance to get beyond that initial draft of your children's picture book manuscript. It serves as a short guide on how to lay out your manuscript to appropriately meet the definition of a children's picture book. It also shows you how to design the book yourself using PowerPoint and then make it ready for publishing on Kindle and CreateSpace.

You will benefit more if you already have some knowledge of using Microsoft Office products. However, I go step by step, so you can follow along even if using Microsoft Office is new for you.

As a thank you for supporting my work, I am offering you a free copy of my children's picture book **Meet**

the Imaginative Joe Dreamer. Just go to the link below to sign up and download the book:

Download free eBook at:

https://forms.aweber.com/form/16/764779816.htm

WHY ME?

So, why should you listen to me for advice on how to self-publish your children's picture book? Let me tell you.

1. Firstly, I have done it myself. Yes, I have self-published a couple of children's picture books that turned out well. They are both available on Amazon. They are **Meet the Imaginative Joe Dreamer** and **Joe Dreamer and His Easter Bunny**.

2. Secondly, I give you access to receiving my children's picture book for free.

3. Thirdly, I am a freelance writer who has been writing for more than 20 years. I have self-published five books thus far.

4. Lastly, from an academic standpoint, I have a Masters' degree in Communication for Social and Behavior Change; and a Certificate in Technical Communication.

I state the above points not to brag in any way, but just to give you some background as to who I am and the reason you should listen to what I have to say about self-publishing your children's picture book.

CHILDREN'S PICTURE BOOK VS. CHILDREN'S STORY BOOK

Yes, there is a difference in producing a children's picture book versus a children's story book. Note the key words here are picture and story. Some children's books are geared at older children. These have fewer pictures and more text.

The other dolls ran after her. They went through the house until they came to the **kitchen** door. "This is the door," said Raggedy Ann. Now all the other dolls could smell something good. They knew it would be very nice to eat.

But none of the dolls were tall enough to open the door. They pulled. They pushed. But the door stayed closed.

The dolls were talking and pulling and pushing. At times one doll would fall down. Then other dolls would climb on her to open the door. But the door wouldn't open. Finally, Raggedy Ann sat down on the floor.

When the other dolls saw Raggedy Ann sitting with her hands on her head, they knew she was thinking.

"Shh, Shh!" they said to each other. They sat quietly in front of her.

"There must be a way to get in the kitchen," said Raggedy Ann.

"Raggedy says there must be a way to get inside," said all the dolls.

"I can't think clearly today," said Raggedy Ann. "It feels like I have a hole in my head."

Lisa ran to Raggedy Ann and took off her cap. "Yes, there is a hole in your head, Raggedy!" she said. Then she took a **needle** from her dress and used it to sew shut the hole in Raggedy's head. "It does not look very good, but I think I closed it!" she said.

"I feel so much better!" said Raggedy Ann happily. "Now I can think clearly."

"Now Raggedy can think clearly!" shouted all the dolls.

"My thoughts were running out of the hole before!" said Raggedy Ann.

"They were running out, Raggedy!" shouted all the other dolls.

"Now that I can think clearly," said Raggedy Ann, "I think the door must be **locked** and to get in we must unlock it with the **key**. See, there is a key in the door!"

Picture books on the other hand, have lots of pictures with less text. They tend to have a picture on each page.

Some books are geared at very small children, such as toddlers, and have even less text on each page. These books have as little as three to five words on a page.

My children's picture book has 25 words or less per page and the text is laid over the picture. There is a picture on every page.

There was a boy named Joe Dreamer, who lived in the Cayman Islands with his Mom and Dad.

So, if you have written a story suited for children, but you are not sure in which category it falls, you can decide based on the amount of text and pictures you intend to include.

The overall word length for children's picture books is usually no more than 800 to 1,000 words. If you have more words than that, then you could be looking at more of a children's story book instead of a picture book.

Use fewer words and more pictures for your younger audience. This is because, in most cases, a younger child has less experience with reading and has a lower attention span than older children.

PLANNING YOUR BOOK

CHILDREN'S PICTURE BOOK DUMMY

If you do decide that it is a children's picture book that you will create, then there are resources that can help you with that process, one of which is the children's picture book dummy.

The children's picture book dummy is like a story board mockup of what your finished book will look like. You can make one yourself. You need eight sheets of plain paper, a pair of scissors and some stick glue, a pencil, and your printed manuscript. There are many examples of this online, so do an online search and see the various samples and templates. Here's one example below. The gray shaded boxes are placeholders for the inside front and back covers.

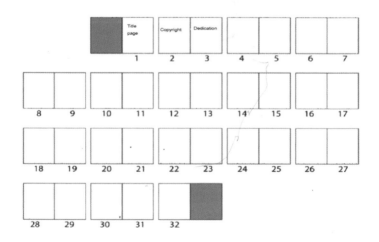

You are trying to achieve a finished book of 32 pages. Bear in mind that your completed book may not be 8 ½ x11 in size. And even if it were, in the event you chose that as the print size, you would still be using only a small fraction of each page for the text. Remember, you are putting 25 words per page or less.

- ❖ So, what you are going to do, is gather eight blank sheets of paper sized 8 ½ x 11.

- ❖ Stack them all together, just the way you would if you were going to place them in a printer.

- ❖ Then fold them in half.

- ❖ Now, go through and number each page. You should get 32 pages in total, which is the standard size for a children's picture book.

- ❖ Then, work out where your text will go.

- ❖ Label out the first few pages in pencil for the title page, copyright page, and, optionally, a dedication page.

- ❖ Cut out the story text from each page of your manuscript and paste it onto your dummy.

This now gives you a visual of how your story is flowing. You can see if any text needs to be moved around or modified in any way.

PAGE TURNERS

One of the things to pay close attention to is how the story ends from one page to the next. Does the content make you eager to know what happens next when you turn the page? The dummy is very useful in helping us determine this.

Similar to novels, when a chapter ends and you are eager to read what comes next, so too does a children's picture book need to grab the readers' attention and leave them eager to turn the page to find out more.

MODIFYING TEXT

The dummy gives you a closer look at your text and how it fits and flows from page to page. You can see whether you need to shift text around to help the story flow better.

You also get to see if the text is too lengthy on some pages and whether there is anything you can cut or re-word.

You get to see what word choices you have used and can determine whether to use simpler words to suit the intended age group.

BOOK LAYOUT

The picture book dummy will help you lay out your book to fit the required guidelines. A standard children's picture book is 32 pages. So, once you paste in your text to the dummy, you will get an idea of whether it all fits into 32 pages.

You should look to include a copyright page and a title page. Some people include two title pages – one full title, and one half-title. This will form your front matter.

FRONT MATTER

As mentioned, your front matter will include the full title page, optionally a half title page, and the copyright page.

The full title page includes the author and illustrator name and usually an image, like the example below.

Meet the Imaginative Joe Dreamer

Written by Karlene Stewart

Illustrated by Telmo Sampaio

The half title page is literally just the title. Preferably the half title page should come just before the full title page. But some experts say it could be the last page before the story begins… It's kind of like pulling away the curtains before the show begins.

YOUR HALF TITLE
HERE

The copyright page will come after the full title page and includes the copyright notice, which is Copyright © the Year, Your Name (similar to the copyright page in this book). You would include the All Rights Reserved verbiage, similar to the one in this book.

Your ISBN details will go on this page as well, and if you would like to include the author's contact details and website information, these would go on this page.

Meet the Imaginative Joe Dreamer
By Karlene Stewart

Copyright © 2015 Karlene Stewart

All Rights Reserved. No part of this publication may be
reproduced, stored in a retrieval system, or transmitted in
any form, without the express consent of the author. The
only exception is by a reviewer, who may quote short
excerpts in a review.

Visit the author's website at
www.karlenestewart.com

Revised edition, 2017

Cover Artwork design by Lisabook

ISBN: 978-1542862684

Printed in the United States of America

If you choose to include a Dedication page, this would come after the Copyright page.

Dedication

I would like to dedicate this book to my two sons, Jamie-Dean and Jason. I hope the book will inspire you to use your wildest imaginations. I love you both so dearly. Thank you for your playful, fun ways.

BODY TEXT

Naturally, you follow through with the story, starting on page four if you go with the three-page front matter, and on page five if you include a dedication page. But, ideally if you are creating a facing-pages book, you would want your story to begin on either page four or six.

BACK MATTER

You may have two pages of back matter; one page for the About the Author information and the other for About the Illustrator. If this is not your first book you could also include a page for Other Works by the Author.

About the Author

Karlene Stewart is the author of several books; *Let My Soul Bare, You Can Rise Up* and *What If...All You Can Imagine*. Karlene holds a Master of Arts degree in Communication for Social and Behavior Change, from the University of the West Indies, Jamaica. She began her published writing during her teenage years as a Youth Writer with Jamaica's national newspaper, *The Gleaner*. Today, Karlene focuses mainly on writing blogs, e-books and short stories.

ILLUSTRATIONS

You can either work with an illustrator or illustrate the book yourself if you have that ability. You could be looking at maybe 27 to 28 illustrations to make the 32-page standard length. Back matter will help make up the page numbers.

FINDING AN ILLUSTRATOR

If you are not able to illustrate your book yourself, then you will likely need to hire an illustrator.

Depending on your budget, you may want to hire a professional illustrator. I would suggest doing some research on the internet and see what is available.

A more affordable option is using a freelance illustrator from www.fiverr.com. You pay a much lower rate per illustration this way. Go to the site and do a search for illustrator. A few options will show up and you can browse through them before making a selection.

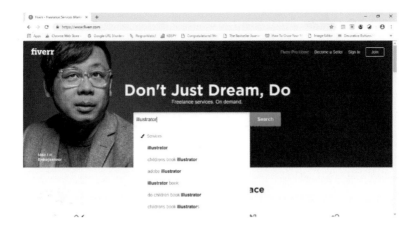

Note however, that you have to sign up and log in before you can place an order. You will note there are various price ranges, so choose the option that best suits your budget and desire.

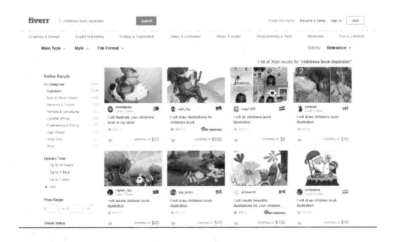

USING IMAGES

Depending on what your story is about and who the characters are, it may be possible for you to access images through the public domain via sites such as Creative Commons.

Just be careful to read the terms of use and make sure you are not infringing on any copyright rules. Whatever images you use in this way should be free to modify and to use commercially, since you are after all producing a book to be sold.

Just do a Google search and you will find the Creative Commons website.

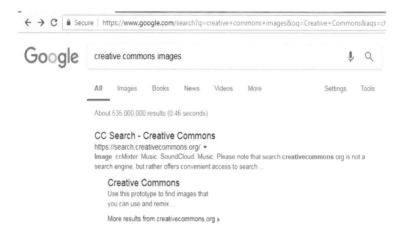

You will see from the below screenshot that it does provide the option in your search to "use for commercial purposes."

TEXT CHOICE AND DESIGN

Let's talk about text for a moment. If you're like me, you may wonder what font to use and what size the text should be? While preparing my first children's picture book, one of my challenges was knowing what font would look most appealing to children.

My first choice was Comic Sans, but then I found out that there is some controversy surrounding this font. Some sources say it makes your work look amateur. The book designer I later chose told me it was not an acceptable children's book font for the interior design. She suggested using either Bookman Old Style or Century Gothic. That's interesting, as these fonts look simple and basic to me. I also notice that on the Kids Book Creator (which we will speak about later), they have Georgia as the only choice. Georgia also looks simple and basic.

A professional book designer will most likely know of the most appropriate and suitable font to use. But, if you are doing this on your own, then the safest choices are the fonts I mentioned above.

There is greater flexibility in choosing the font for your front cover. You may use up to two different fonts on the cover.

As far as the text size, there is some flexibility here also. Have a look through a few children's picture books. Some have text sizes of 11 or 12 inches, but you do have some that are larger and even bolded for greater emphasis. It all depends on your book design choice and what you are aiming to convey. For example, if you are aiming for a bit of comic effect while demonstrating a dog barking, you could show this as **RUFF**, **RUFF**.

On the back cover, the body text is usually smaller than the front cover and is mainly paragraph style, as in the below example.

Meet the Imaginative
Joe Dreamer

Meet the Imaginative Joe Dreamer is the first in a series of children's picture books, introducing a young boy, who channels his frustrations into his creative passions - drawing and his imagination. In this first edition, Joe faces the challenge of going to the beach on a rainy day.

The book is set in the beautiful Cayman Islands, where Joe resides with his parents. Joe's parents are entertained by his creativity and sense of humor. Similarly, the book serves to encourage young children to be creative and imaginative. Older children may read alone, or younger children may have their parents read to them. This cozy picture book, is a great read for any family, as it brings together exciting ingredients of the Caribbean, imagination, and viewing problem solving through a young child's eyes.

Karlene Stewart is the author of several books: Let My Soul Bare, You Can Rise Up and What If... All You Can Imagine. Karlene holds a Master of Arts degree in Communication for Social and Behavior Change, from the University of the West Indies, Jamaica. She began her published writing during her teenage years as a Youth Writer with Jamaica's national newspaper, The Gleaner. Today, Karlene focuses mainly on writing blogs, e-books and short stories.

www.karlenestewart.com

ISBN 978-1-5428-6268-4

9 781542 862684

DESIGNING YOUR BOOK

So, now you have all your text and illustrations ready to go. But how do you put it all together and have it look like a book?

CHOOSE YOUR SOFTWARE

Guess what? You don't need to hire a professional book designer if you don't want to, or can't afford to. You also don't need to try your hand at InDesign or Photoshop. You can design your book using Microsoft PowerPoint.

If you don't have this software, I suggest you go ahead and purchase a Microsoft Office option that includes PowerPoint.

Do a Google search? Then click one of the options for either Microsoft Office or 365 Office. It asks for a login because, once you make a purchase, you can activate via your Hotmail/Microsoft account. As you will see from the below screenshot, you get different buying choices, so read through each and choose the option that best suits you.

All   News   Images   Books   More   Settings   Tools

About 705,000,000 results (0.59 seconds)

Ask Microsoft Office Support | A Tech Will Answer You Now
[Ad] www.justanswer.com/Microsoft/Office ▾
★★★★★ Rating for justanswer.com: 4.9 - 2,117 reviews
Get 1-on-1 Help with your device. Get **Microsoft** Answers Online & Save Time! Helped Over 8MM
Worldwide. 12MM+ Questions Answered. Services: Remote Tech Support, Fast Online Repairs,
Microsoft Tech Experts, All **Microsoft** Programs, Troubleshooting.

Microsoft Office Help   **Office 365 Assistance**
Get Connected to a Microsoft Tech!   Office 365 Experts are Waiting
Questions Answered Every 9 Minutes.   to Answer Your Questions ASAP.

Microsoft Office | Productivity Tools for Home & Office
https://products.office.com/en-us/home ▾
From desktop to web for Macs and PCs, Office delivers the tools to get work ...

Office 365 Login | Microsoft Office
https://www.office.com/ ▾
Collaborate for free with online versions of **Microsoft** Word, PowerPoint, Excel, and OneNote. Save
documents, spreadsheets, and presentations online, ...
Office Products · Get the most from Office with ... · Microsoft Office Support · Android

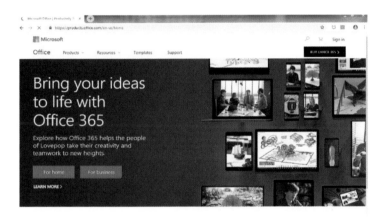

What is Office 365

Office 365 is a cloud-based subscription service that brings together the best
tools for the way people work today. By combining best-in-class apps like
Excel and Outlook with powerful cloud services like OneDrive and Microsoft
Teams, Office 365 lets anyone create and share anywhere on any device.

Learn more about Office 365

HOME ⟩ SMALL BUSINESS ⟩ ENTERPRISE ⟩ EDUCATION ⟩

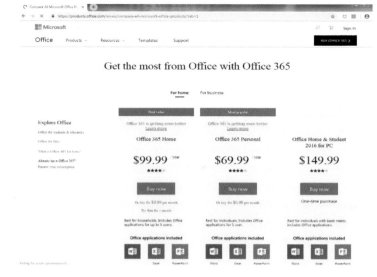

WORKING WITH POWERPOINT

PAGE DESIGN/LAYOUT

Using PowerPoint is straightforward. If you are accustomed to using Microsoft Word, then the interface of PowerPoint will be familiar. The "Insert" tab is what you will use the most. You will insert new slides, pictures, and text. There is also the option to insert shapes and add colors, similar to how you would in Microsoft Word. I have prepared a few screenshots to give you an idea.

In the below screenshots you see the option to Insert new slides.

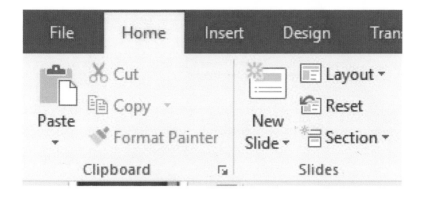

A new blank slide will look like the one below. You just need to edit accordingly.

If you click on the slide box you will notice it creates a few circles around the border. When this happens, you are able to delete the box altogether. You can do this when you plan to put images on the page directly, before adding the text.

This is what your slide with an inserted image looks like.

And now with text added:

Here is some text added next to my mouse image. I have put my text to fall in line with my image. I can have my text above if I want also, or I can add my text below.

You have the option to resize your images. When you insert an image, it may show up larger than you would like. So, what you can do is click the image box until you see circles form around it. Move your cursor to one of the corners and drag either in to go smaller or out to go larger.

You can also design your page with your image going fully across the page/slide. This is known as Bleed or Full Bleed.

Usually in this format, you would add the text directly over the image as opposed to beside, above, or below it.

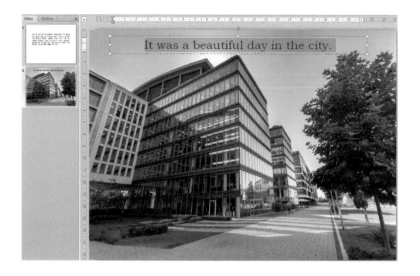

You can also experiment with adding colors, shapes, and shape effects to your backgrounds.

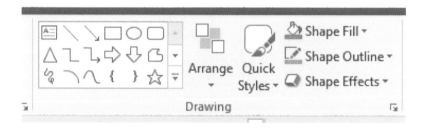

You have to click on your text box or image box in order for the picture or shape effect options to show up for you to access. The shape and picture icons fall under the Format tab on the top menu bar.

In the first screenshot below I have added a border around my image.

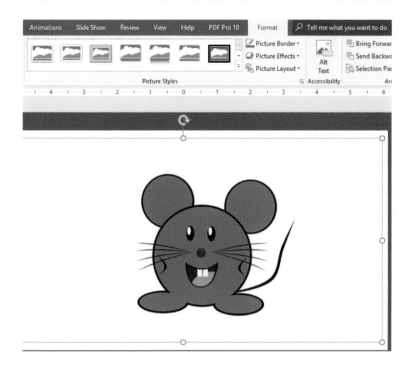

In the next image I did a 3D shape effect with the text.

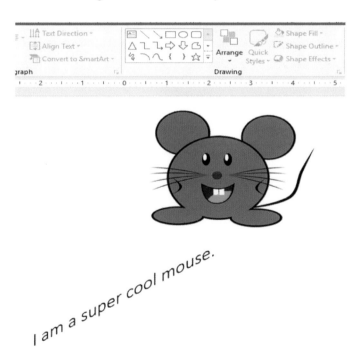

I am a super cool mouse.

You may even use the Design Ideas tab to the right for a quick selection of design styles choices.

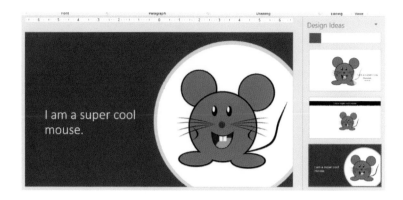

Just have a look around PowerPoint and test things out on your own. Get creative and see what works best for you.

As for the front and back matter, these are largely just text, so it should be OK to just copy and paste those texts from your picture book manuscript into the relevant places before and after your story.

You are well on your way now to self-publishing your children's picture book.

Hopefully, you have decided on the size you would like your book to be and whether landscape or portrait layout. You can choose these settings in PowerPoint. I'll show you how.

Go to the design tab in the tools menu, which is to your far left. Then look to your far right for the tab that says Slide Size and has a drop-down arrow.

Click the drop-down arrow by the "Slide Size." You will see it gives the option for wide screen and standard. If you look below that, you will see the option for "Custom Size." Go ahead and click that.

You can either choose Widescreen or Standard from the drop down menu; then click Portrait or Landscape. You will see your file size change.

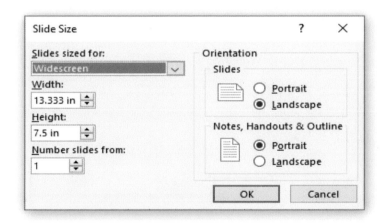

BOOK COVER DESIGN

The final item you will need before saving and uploading for publishing is a book cover. There are various options for that. Again, you can purchase this for a very affordable price on www.fiverr.com.

You can design a cover in PowerPoint, if it is just an eBook. You can design one within Kindle Direct Publishing and/or you can design one within CreateSpace. There are many possibilities, so it will be up to you to explore and see what works best for your time and budget.

If you would like to design a cover yourself using PowerPoint, here's how you could do that:

First go to the File tab and scroll down for New. Go ahead and click on that. You should see a few slide options, such as in the screenshot below. Choose one that you would like to work with.

For demonstration purposes, I have selected the first blue option in the list, called Circuit.

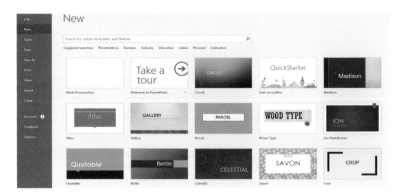

Notice it says to add title and subtitle. Go ahead and type those in: type the title of your book and your subtitle. If there is no subtitle you may use that box to add your author name.

You should have something that looks like the below image. You can now modify it as you feel fit, by changing the background color or adding a picture if you'd like to.

Here's what it looks like now with a picture added. It's simple, but decent. I have used the Slide Size settings to make the cover size Portrait. While we are on the subject of size, I should note that Kindle will require the cover image size to be at least 1,000 pixels long and 625 pixels wide. You would use a nicer photo or illustration on your cover than what I have used to demonstrate here, but at least you can see the possibilities. Of course, if you want something more professional looking, you can go that route as well.

Once your cover is ready, you can go ahead with converting and publishing, as I explain next.

CONVERTING YOUR FILE

So, when you design your book in PowerPoint and save it, it gets saved with the extension .ppt. Next you need to save a copy as a .pdf file. So, go to File, which will take you to a screen that looks like the below screen shot. Then scroll down to Export and click on Create PDF Document. Save the document on your desktop or in a location on your computer where it is easy to find it later.

WORKING WITH KINDLE KIDS BOOK CREATOR

Next, you have the option to either upload your book on Kindle Direct Publishing as a PDF document, or you can first convert it to a .mobi file

A PDF document is acceptable, but the quality may not be great. So, I recommend that you convert it to .mobi,, which converts better and produces a higher quality book version.

You can do so using the Kindle Kids Book Creator. You need to download it online and follow the instructions that come with it. Below is what the icon looks like.

If you already have an Amazon KDP account, you can sign in and go to the Help menu and then look to the far left of the page for Publishing Process. Then scroll down to Publishing Illustrated Books. Once there, you will find Kindle Kids Book Creator as one of the options. You can go ahead and download either the Mac or Windows PC version.

Once you have Kindle Kids Book Creator up and running, you will upload your file and save it for publishing. Once your file is saved for publishing, it will create a .mobi file. Just take note of where the file is being saved, because you will need to go to that location when you are ready to upload the .mobi file to Kindle Direct Publishing.

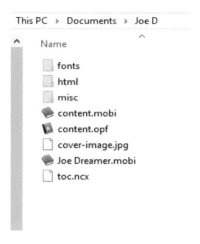

Although two .mobi files show up, upload the one that is named with the title you used to save your file. In this case mine is named Joe Dreamer.mobi. It appears to me that both that file and the content.mobi files have the same content.

Here is an image to give you an idea of what the Kindle Kids Book Creator looks like and how to navigate it. You will notice at the top left corner when you open it, that there is a User Guide within the help menu. Go ahead and download it.

Now, if you look at the bottom you will notice there are two options – one to create a new kid's book, and another to open an existing book. If you are new to using Kindle Kids Book Creator, you can go ahead and click the option to Create a New Kid's Book.

From there you will see step-by-step instructions that walk you through the entire process. But if you get a bit stuck, you have the User Guide handy as well.

I will go through a few of the features with you. First, once you hit the tab to create a new book, you will be taken to a screen that explains the steps you need to do in sequence.

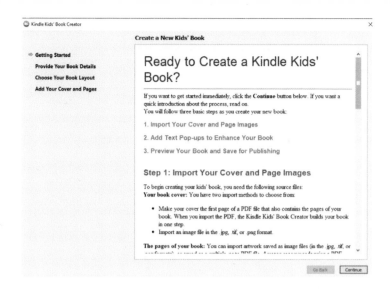

You will be given the option to import your cover and inside pages as one complete document. Or, alternatively, you can insert each of your .jpeg images one at a time, using the Add Page feature.

Create a New Kids' Book

Step 1: Import Your Cover and Page Images

To begin creating your kids' book, you need the following source files:

Your book cover: You have two import methods to choose from:

- Make your cover the first page of a PDF file that also contains the pages of your book. When you import the PDF, the Kindle Kids' Book Creator builds your book in one step.
- Import an image file in the .jpg, .tif, or .png format.

The pages of your book: You can import artwork saved as image files (in the .jpg, .tif, or .png formats), or saved as a multiple-page PDF file. Amazon recommends using a PDF because you can import your cover and your pages in one step and the page order is set by the PDF.

TIP: If you plan to import multiple images simultaneously, Amazon recommends that you number your image filenames sequentially because the Kindle Kids' Book Creator adds images to your book in alphabetical order based on filename. For example, "Page 01.jpg," and "Page 02.jpg" will produce better results than "Title Page.jpg" and "Copyright.jpg."

If you go with the first option, you will end up with a screen looking like the below image.

If you go with the second option, you will end up with a screen looking like the below image.

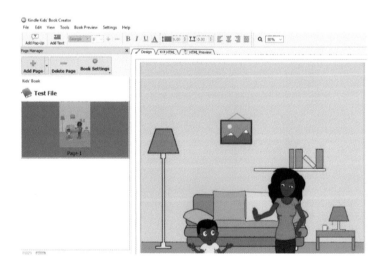

You will notice you can add text. Georgia is the only available preloaded font, but you can add additional fonts by going to Tools + Add Font. You would pull up any other fonts you have already saved to your computer, such as fonts you downloaded from the Internet.

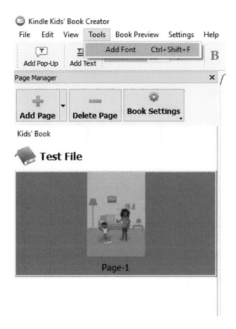

This option is good if you are designing directly in Kids Book Creator and doing a text -over- image layout. Use the Add Text menu to create the text box over the image/illustration.

You even get to choose languages other than English. I have not used this option, but should you choose to publish your book in Spanish, for instance, Kids Book Creator gives you this option.

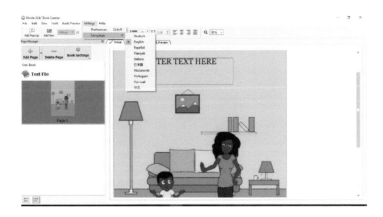

But, if you have already designed your book using PowerPoint, I recommend you go with the first option where you upload your cover and interior file as one complete document, because you are only now trying to convert your book into a .mobi file format. Once your file is fully compiled, you go to the File menu and choose Save for Publishing.

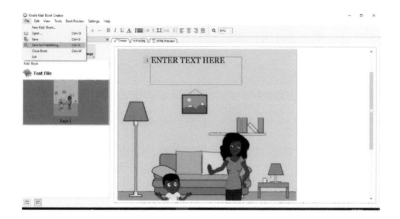

PUBLISHING

KINDLE DIRECT PUBLISHING (KDP)

KINDLE EBOOK

Look for Kindle Direct Publishing online and follow the instructions. You can sign up with your Amazon account login information. Or if you do not yet have an Amazon account, you can go ahead and sign up for one. The KDP site is at: https://kdp.amazon.com/en_US/

The interface is user friendly, but I will explain how to navigate it with a few illustrations. The site walks you through the process. It is pretty much like filling out an online form. A few things you need to have handy are the book description and up to seven keywords. You will be asked to enter that information. The keywords should be words that will help customers find your book when they do a search on Amazon.

Once you have signed in you will see the option for creating a new kindle book title. Go ahead and click that. There is also now the option to create a paperback using KDP. That is a new feature on KDP, which I discuss shortly.

After clicking on Kindle eBook, under Creating a New Title, you will be taken to a page that shows you the next steps you need to complete. These will be displayed across three main tabs. Click them in order and complete the steps.

As mentioned earlier, you need to have your book description and keyword details at hand. You need to enter these on the first Kindle eBook Details tab.

What is very good about KDP is that throughout it there are links that explain how to use its features, in the event you are unclear about something. Here is an example.

Enter up to 7 search keywords that describe your book. How do I choose keywords? ▾

Description   This will appear on your book's Amazon detail page. Why do book descriptions matter? ▾

<h2> Joe Dreamer at Easter</h2>
<b> Joe Dreamer loves to color and draw, but what will he do if his materials are not available to him? How will he handle the challenges that face him?</b>

3376
characters left

If you are familiar with HTML you can enter your description in HTML format, which is what I have done in the example above. If not, don't worry about it; you can enter your description in regular text. My choice for HTML was just so some text stands out more.

You also need to choose what are known as Categories. These are broad areas under which people would search for your book.

Categories   Choose up to two browse categories. Why are categories important? ▾

Juvenile Fiction > Animals > Rabbits
Juvenile Fiction > Holidays & Celebrations > Easter & Lent

Set Categories

In the eBook Content tab section, you will be asked to upload your manuscript. You will note that you are told the various formats that are available to you. So, choose only one of the recommended suggestions.

Go ahead and click the link to the right that says, "See a full list here." This list shows the pros and cons for using a certain format.

Click on the various formats and you will see details to help you determine whether to use that format or not. For example, here is what Word format shows.

After uploading your manuscript, you will need to upload your cover.

You can use KDP's cover creator. If going this route, you will need to have a cover image ready. Or you may choose a cover image from KDP's stock images.

Kindle eBook
Cover

You can create a cover using our Cover Creator tool or upload your own Kindle eBook cover. See our cover guidelines.

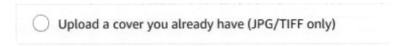

Your other option is to have your cover professionally designed. If you do this it has to be JPG or TIFF format only.

⭕ Upload a cover you already have (JPG/TIFF only)

Now your book is all ready for publishing, but you can preview it before hitting the publish button. Just hit launch previewer and you will see what your book will look like on a kindle device.

The final thing you will be asked about in this tab section is ISBN. You don't have to use an ISBN for a Kindle book.

But you can use one if you choose to. You can click the link on KDP that tells you a bit about ISBN. I say more on this when we discuss the print book version.

You will Save and Continue to the final tab section. There you will select your book's price and see how much royalty you will be paid accordingly. Your book must be priced for at least $2.99 to get a 75% royalty. If lower than $2.99 then you qualify for the 35% royalty.

Once you've selected your price and answered all other questions on that page then you will accept the terms and conditions, and go ahead with submitting your book for publishing.

Terms & Conditions

It can take up to 72 hours for your title to be available for purchase on Amazon.

By clicking Publish below, I confirm that I have all rights necessary to make the content I am uploading available for marketing, distribution and sale in each territory I have indicated above, and that I am in compliance with the KDP Terms and Conditions.

| < Back to Content | Save as Draft | Publish Your Kindle eBook |

Once you complete all the steps on KDP, you should then have a Kindle book created, which will go live on Amazon within 24 to 72 hours. In my experience, it usually shows up within about 12 hours. It's fine if you want to settle with just a kindle version of your book, but children's books also work great for print. If you would like to create a print version, then you will use another online program called CreateSpace to do so.

KDP PRINT BOOK

Previously self-publishers were using CreateSpace to publish their print books and Kindle Direct Publishing was used only for publishing the Kindle eBook version. Since this publication, I have used the KDP interface to publish my print book and I do like it. It's very easy to understand and there are only few quick steps.

Click the Paperback tab and go through the steps that follow.

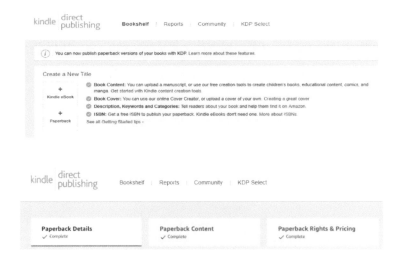

You will come to three main screens broken out according to your book details, content, and pricing details.

The process is very similar to that of the eBook upload.

You are asked to enter the book's trim size, paper type, and whether you will have your images bleed or not.

Print Options   The default options selected below are based on the most common selections. How will printing cost be calculated? *

Interior & paper type
What ink and paper types does KDP support? *

Black & white interior with cream paper	Black & white interior with white paper	Color interior with white paper

(i) You cannot change your Interior & paper type after your book has been published.

Trim Size
What is a trim size? *

6 x 9 in 15.24 x 22.86 cm	Select a different size

(i) You can not change your trim size once your book has been published

Bleed Settings
What are bleed settings? *

No Bleed	Bleed

Bleed refers to if your images extend to the edges of the page. Below is what a bleed page looks like.

When the image is surrounded by white space, there is no bleed, as in the below example.

Now you are ready for the book Contents section, where you will upload your book interior pages and cover page.

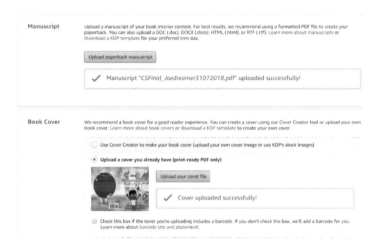

You will recall being asked about ISBN for the Kindle version, which is optional there. However, in the print setup this is mandatory. You can use a free KDP assigned version, or you may purchase your own.

ISBN stands for International Standard Book Numbers. It is a unique 10- or 13-digit number that is assigned to every published print book. You can use a KDP-assigned ISBN for free or you can buy your own. Bowker Identifier Services is the main provider through which to purchase an ISBN.

There must be space on your book's back cover to add the ISBN barcode. This space needs to be at least 2 inches wide and 1.2 inches tall.

For the final tab section, you then get to choose your distribution markets and set your price. Your potential royalty is automatically calculated based on your book's price.

Your book is now ready for publishing, but you have the option of reviewing a proof copy first. As KDP is owned by Amazon, you would order this proof as an Amazon purchase, but at a price that is heavily reduced from the normal retail price.

Once you are happy with your proof, you're all set to publish.

CREATESPACE

FORMATTING FOR CREATESPACE

CreateSpace is another publishing platform for print books. Before using CreateSpace however, you may want to make sure that your book size matches CreateSpace requirements. Let's use the example of a 6x9 book. To allow for cropping, you will need a 6.25 x 9.25 book size. The extra .25 inches give room for cropping, so that images or text close to the edge are not cut off.

To format your book for CreateSpace, you can go back to PowerPoint and save another version of your file, but this time choose your Slide Size custom size as 6.25 x 9.25, then hit OK. If you have a differently sized book, just add the .25. You will then be taken to a screen asking you to Maximize or Ensure Fit. Choose Maximize.

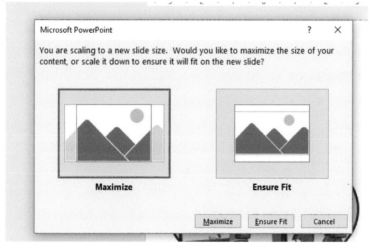

Should you have any difficulty with the formatting, you can hire a freelancer on Fiverr who has CreateSpace formatting experience. Just do a search on that site. To make an order however, you need to sign up and log in.

Now go to the CreateSpace website at:

https://www.createspace.com.

Sign up by creating a user name and password. Your Amazon account details may not work there.

Once you have logged in, you will be taken to the Member Dashboard area, where there is a prompt for you to Add New Title. Go ahead and click that.

You will then be taken to a screen similar to KDP, where you do a walkthrough. There is an option for a "Guided" or "Expert" set-up process. Choose Guided.

Go through the required steps.

A lot of the steps are similar to what you see on KDP. You will need to have your cover, your book description and some keywords at hand, but, in this case, you will need just five keywords instead of seven.

The first step asks for the Title of your book. Next is the ISBN.

The Interior pages tab allows you to search for your PDF file and then choose your trim size and the color type. Picture books are usually full color and on white paper.

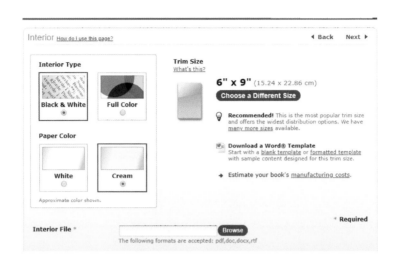

Once you save, you will get a chance to preview and see if your book looks like what you intended. Whatever is within the dotted line gets printed and whatever is outside the dotted line may get cropped.

Once you are happy with your interior, you can work on your cover upload. You either upload your PDF cover, or you can try building one from scratch using the CreateSpace interface. I prefer uploading a cover. You have a choice between a gloss cover or a matte cover.

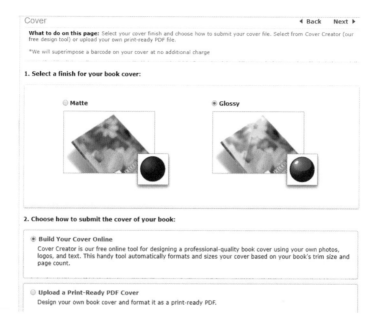

One of the things you will find that's somewhat different in CreateSpace compared to KDP are the Channels. Channels help you select where your book will be distributed. There are similarities to KDP to the extent that in KDP you choose marketing territories, but CreateSpace also includes distribution to libraries and academic institutions.

CreateSpace Channels

There is no cost associated with having your book distributed across Amazon in the United States, Amazon Europe, and the CreateSpace e-store.

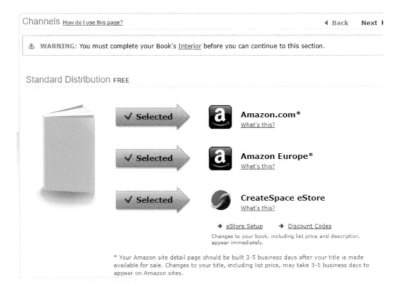

There is also no charge for you to have your book distributed to libraries and academic institutions. This is a good deal, because your book has a wide reach without you doing much marketing.

Once you go through every section and complete it as requested, you will have the option to preview your final book. Once you are satisfied with it, you will be given an option to order the proof. You may review a digital proof, or you can pay for a physical proof copy of the book to be shipped to you. Here's a view of a couple pages of my digital proof. Once you are happy with the proof, go ahead and approve it for publishing. Any issues will be communicated to you by the CreateSpace technical team; if not, your book will be published.

Meet the Imaginative
Joe Dreamer

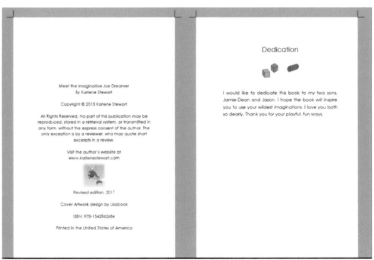

YOU'RE PUBLISHED

You should now have your book available for sale on Amazon in both the print and kindle eBook formats.

Congratulations, you have just self-published your children's picture book. This is a big achievement and you should feel proud of yourself.

Thank You

I hope that this book was useful to you. Hopefully, you are now a bit clearer on how to approach self-publishing your children's book. If so, I would be very grateful if you would kindly leave me a short review. Your support really does make a difference and I read all the reviews personally, so I can get your feedback and make this book even better.

Thank you for your support. Remember you can receive a gift from me by signing up through the link below to get a free copy of my children's picture book **Meet the Imaginative Joe Dreamer**.

Download free eBook at:

https://forms.aweber.com/form/16/764779816.htm

ABOUT THE AUTHOR

Karlene K. Stewart is a blogger and writer of both fiction and non-fiction, who lives in the sunny Cayman Islands. Her many books include philosophical and inspirational titles, but her latest offering is for young children, with the exciting **Meet the Imaginative Joe Dreamer**, which is aimed at helping young children learn how to problem solve and build up their confidence.

Her influences come from her favorite authors: the inspirational writer Joel Osteen and the ever-popular writer of children's literature, Dr. Seuss. She plans to continue with her eclectic titles with follow-up books in the near future.

Director 365   DRAGON = ?

Paint Shop PRO 2022

        ULTIMATE =

Printed in Great Britain
by Amazon

70358896R00039